Books by Dennis M Keating

The Olympics:
An Unauthorized Unsanctioned History
*
Charlie Whitman
Was a Friend of Mine
*
Ena Road
*
The Fulda Gap
*
A Chicago Tale
*
Black Lahu
*
Poetry for Men

A
Chicago Tale

Murder in the City

Dennis M Keating

This book was created by
the Golden Sphere team
in coordination with the Honolulu Guy,
Dennis M Keating

Copyright © 2017 Dennis M Keating
ISBN-13: 978-1-63538-004 – 0
ISBN-10: 1-63538-004 – 9

The Author

Dennis M Keating

The Honolulu Guy

DEDICATION

To the men and women who serve and protect the city of Chicago

ACKNOWLEDMENTS

Thanks to

Professor Steven Taylor Goldsberry
My Mentor

Paula Marie Fernandez and Hikari Kimura
For Artwork and Maps

Gail M Baugniet and Faith Scheideman
Advisors and Proofreaders

Sandy
My Wife, Proponent and Ally

A

Chicago Tale

A Narrative Poem written in Rhyming Couplets

BY

DENNIS M KEATING

Dennis M Keating, the author of **A Chicago Tale,** has enjoyed a rather peripatetic life. His stories reflect this as each takes place in a different locale – Germany, Thailand, Hawaii, Texas and Chicago.

All five stories are true. Four relate to Keating's personal experiences. The fifth took place almost ninety years ago, but its initial incident occurred just a half block from Keating's current home.

The stories are written for male audiences as they include action, adventure and/or murder in their central themes. They are written in a poetic, rhyming couplet format. Hopefully, this will encourage more men to develop an interest in verse and thereby expand the realm of poetry.

While these tales include gritty elements, many women will also appreciate them. Trustfully, all audiences will find them interesting and compelling.

Dennis M Keating joined the staff of the Superintendent of Police in the fall of 1965. He remained with the police for four years, until 1969. Keating was a civilian, not a patrolman. He did not wear a uniform nor carry a gun. However, his civilian staff position afforded him a very unique secondary seat in the inner circle of the Chicago Police leadership. This tale concerns one of his experiences during his four years with the Police Department.

 To better understand the situation, during the 1960's, the Chicago Police Department underwent a major administration shift. This change was preceded by a police scandal that even by Chicago standards was too big to ignore. Due to this scandal, Richard J. Daley, the powerful mayor of Chicago, was forced to bring in an outsider, Orlando W. Wilson, to clean up the mess.

Wilson was not your ordinary police chief. He had a PhD in Police Administration, as well as a Harvard and Berkeley background. He also had one other feather in his hat. After World War II, Wilson oversaw the denazification of the German police. The skills he learned in post war Berlin served him well in rough and tumble Chicago. Wilson was given Carte Blanche freedom. Daley ordered the Ward bosses and Aldermen to keep their hands off. With this guideline, Wilson hired individuals based on their academic and intellectual abilities rather than their political clout. Many recent university graduates were hired into police headquarters. The building took on a fresher, younger look. The author was one of these newcomers.

In the Ghetto

In January 1969, Elvis Presley recorded the song, *In the Ghetto*. The song has a haunting beginning: "As the snow flies, on a cold and gray Chicago morning," and a tough conclusion: "an angry young man, face down on the street with a gun in his hand."

Three years earlier, in January 1966, on a cold and gray Chicago afternoon, young Donald Dean Jackson entered Fohrman Motors, a ghetto automobile dealership on the west side of Chicago. Jackson was carrying a concealed sawed-off shotgun. To the best of my memory, this is how it went down.

We Serve And Protect

Motto of the Chicago Police

I'd joined the CPD
three months before,

My desk, a few steps
from the Old Man's door.

On the fourth floor
at the old 11th and State.

A pretty good job
with some political weight.

I'd married recently.
My wife, from out of state.

Twice, nightmares woke her.
Guns and death: a policeman's fate.

CPD – The Chicago Police Department, is the second largest, after New York City, non-federal law enforcement agency in the USA. The CPD has 12,000+ police officers and around 2,000 civilian staff.

The Old Man – Orlando W. Wilson, the Police Superintendent (1960 to 1967). Wilson moved his office out of City Hall, to get away from the politicians, ward bosses and aldermen. He relocated to the fourth floor of the building that housed the central police units that served the twenty-one police districts in the city. These central units included the crime lab, the communication center and the evidence room. This building's nickname came from the cross streets where it was located: *11th & State.*

Wilson shared the Superintendent's suite with his top aides. In addition, Wilson's financial staff, including Keating, had offices in the suite.

I told her, "Don't worry,
I'm not a street cop.

No uniform. No gun. Just # 2 Guy
in the Finance Shop."

One day my boss waved me in,
As he's hanging up a call.

His face cold and emotionless.
That's all.

Staring at his desk,
he spoke in a solemn tone;

"Duffy, upstairs."
 He pointed at the phone.

"Don't know the facts yet,"
he said.
"Jolene in Keypunch.
Her brother's been shot dead.

Go stay with her,
until it's all done.

Get her home safe.
Keep her away from everyone."

Jolene was sobbing loudly,
the other keypunchers all sad.

"I tried to stop him," she said,
"from turning bad!"

```
┌─────────────────────────────────────────┐
│                                         │
│   Chicago Police Headquarters           │
│                                         │
│       1121 S. State Street              │
│                                         │
└─────────────────────────────────────────┘
```

The Chicago Police Headquarters was located at 1121 S. State Street, from the beginning of the 1960's until the end of the 1990's.

Her tearful words
flooded across the room.

"I knew something terrible
would be his doom"

"Jolene, I'm sorry."
I spoke very low.

"Let's go next door
'til the detectives show.

They'll need a statement
from you.

I'll drive you home
when it's all through."

In the 1960's, the Chicago Police, like most organizations at the time, employed a large number of keypunch operators, or keypunchers, to enter data into the computers. At the Chicago Police Headquarters, the keypunchers were located together in a large keypunch room. Most of the keypunchers were fulltime employees of the Computer Division. However, three keypunchers were employees of the Finance Division. These three keypunchers, of which Jolene was one, processed all the Police payroll data. Their leader reported to Keating.

Two detectives entered,
after a few minutes went by;

One questioned Jolene; the other
gave me the who, what, why.

Jolene's brother, Donald Dean Jackson,
had a long rap sheet.

An ex-con, six months out of Pontiac,
and back on the street.

 Jackson'd bought a new Caddy
for a thousand down;

Then hidden fees and high interest
made him drown.

Rap Sheet – Slang term used to describe a listing of an individual's criminal records.

An Ex-con – An ex-convict. Someone who has served time in prison for a criminal offense.

Pontiac - This notorious prison is located 100 miles south of Chicago. The Pontiac Correctional Center houses many of Chicago's worst Gangbangers. The 1973 and 1979 Pontiac Riots that killed both guards and prisoners were due to fighting between the Chicago street gangs.

Caddy - A Cadillac automobile. A popular set of wheels for ghetto pimps & hustlers during the 1960s.

"A Cadillac dealer
in a ghetto neighborhood."

Just those few words

didn't sound good.

He purchased the car

less than a month ago;

Each night, he went cruising

with a new bimbo.

On the street,
the Caddy was his tool.

Lookin' in its mirror,
"Oh God, I'm Mr. Joe Cool."

Chicago, as well as much of America, experienced great economic growth and middle class affluence in the late 1940's and 1950's. Most homes had at least one television by the mid 1950's. There were many first-time home owners who chose to relocate to the suburbs of the city.

Fohrman Motors was an automobile agency on Chicago's Westside. Fohrman Motors had become quite well known during the early 1950's because of its aggressive use of local television advertising. During the late 1950's and early 1960's, many white families chose to move to the suburbs, and a white flight void was created. This void was filled by lower income black families and the Westside quickly transitioned into a black ghetto. Fohrman Motors lost its citywide popularity and became known as a ghetto automobile dealership.

Then, a fender bender;
the car needed minor repair.

Mr. Cool's relation with the
dealer went ice cold from there.

He brought the car in
to get the fix-up done.

The salesman was curt.
"We have a problem, son."

"You don't get the car back
until more money's paid.

Read the contract's fine print.
That's how it was made."

Bimbo – A slang term for a young woman who appears physically attractive but is intellectually shallow.

Fender Bender – A minor traffic accident where the damage to the automobiles is minor.

Jackson flared inside.
"Fuck that shit.

You ain't gettin' a dime
til I'm driving it."

The standoff went on for several days.

Nothing was done.

Then Jackson walks in;

under his coat, a sawed-off shotgun.

"Hey, Mr. Salesman,
my car ready yet?"

"If you ain't got cash,
just turn 'round and get."

Fohrman Motors – 1960's era.

Location: 2700 W. Madison Street, Chicago, IL.

Fohrman Motors was founded in 1912 by Benjamin Fohrman the father of Sidney and Edward Fohrman.

With those words,

out comes the gun.

One quick trigger pull;

the salesman was done.

Seeing this, the two Fohrman brothers
bolted for the door.

Blam! Blam! Blood and guts flew.
Their bodies hit the floor.

Nearby, two robbery detectives
were cruising their beat,

They saw the car dealer employees

fleeing into the street.

Sawed-Off Shotgun - Normally the barrel of the shotgun is shortened to less than 18 inches and the stock is also shortened. This makes the shotgun easy to transport and conceal while affording much more powerful firepower than the normal pistol. These features make it a desirable weapon for big city criminals.

"The first shot from a sawed-off shotgun can cut you in half. The second shot can cut you into pieces. "– A Police Officer

Cruising their beat – Typically, police officers are assigned to patrol specific geographic areas of the city, these areas are called their beats.

Pulling their revolvers,
one made a quick guess:

"It's show time, partner.
Robbery in progress."

Detective Anderson took the front,
Detective Charles the side.

They hoped to circle the shooter

and leave him nowhere to hide.

Jackson fired at Andy,
then ducked to reload.

With this, Charles sprang
into fast-forward mode.

A Sawed – Off Shotgun

Charles, on the run,
shot his very best.

The first two slugs
went straight to Jackson's chest.

Then Charles emptied his .38
in the back of Jackson's head.

There was no doubt,
Donald Dean was 100% dead.

Charles nodded to Anderson;
all was through.

Once again, they'd covered each other.
That's what partners do.

A Police Snubnose .38.

A .38 can do the job, but it lacks the power punch of a sawed-off shotgun.

Their adrenaline rushes subsided,
along with their fear.

Next, the paperwork. Then, a bar,
for quick shots chased by beer.

Back at headquarters,
the detective finished updating me.

"Now we go to the morgue.
We need a positive ID."

I looked at Jolene,
all swelled and teary eyed.

Gaining composure, she nodded,
she was ready to ride.

Cook County - The Illinois county where the city of Chicago is located. Cook County is the second most populous county in America after Los Angeles County and more populous than 29 of the 50 states.

Cook County Morgue - From the 1850s to the present day, the morgue has had a well-deserved, notorious reputation. for political patronage, unqualified and unskilled management, and a steady stream of lost bodies.

Political Patronage - Giving a job to an unqualified worker purely because he or she has a relative who has influence or connections. In Chicago, the term for political connections is "clout." Also, a common inquiry about someone's clout is, "Who's your Chinaman?" This is not a derogatory statement. Rather, it means, who is the unknown, behind the scene power broker, who got you your job?

The Old Cook County Morgue
was a disgusting place to go,

Nothing like a Crime Lab

on some CSI TV Show.

Once a Pre-Civil War hospital,
now, some hundred years old.

No upkeep money. All the jobs,

political patronage controlled.

The building's wooden entrance:
Dirty and grotesque.

Inside, an unshaven guy, chomping
a tamale at a cluttered desk.

Cook County Morgue

His food-stained shirt
appeared unchanged for a week.

He had a greasy, gooey glob
dripping down from his cheek.

His ear to a phone,
he was silent for a bit.

Then, suddenly, he barks,
"Stop your fucking shit."

"I don't know where the body is,
and don't give a rat's ass.

Tell your problem to the priest
next Sunday at mass."

Tamale – A popular Chicago snack of Mexican origin. At the time, tamales were often sold at street corner stands.

Coon – A derogatory, slang term for an African American

Ward Boss – For political purposes, Chicago is divided into fifty wards. The ward boss may be the elected alderman or the less visible behind the scenes, but very powerful, ward committeeman. Typically, in Chicago, virtually all the ward bosses are democrats and have control over patronage job appointments.

Hocker – Slang term for a mucus snot

Clipped - Killed

"I got a dozen unclaimed coons
lying in the basement vault.
If a couple got misplaced,
it ain't my goddamn fault.

Don't waste my fucking time
with your fuckin' loss.
If you don't like it, call my uncle.
He's the Ward Boss."

He had stared at us,
when we walked through the door.
Now, with an open-mouth cough,
he spits a hocker on the floor.

Three Fohrman Motors Employees

RIP – On January 7th, 1966
All killed by Donald Dean Jackson.

Albert Sizer, Age 64 – Salesman
Sidney Fohrman, Age 49 – Part Owner
Edward Fohrman, Age 42 – Part Owner

Shortly after the killing, the fifty-year-old Fohrman Motors dealership chose to permanently shutter its doors.

When he sees we're the cops,
he shrugs with a frown.

Then he stares at Jolene's breasts.
His tongue makes a clucking sound.

The detective was curt: "We wanna
see the guy the cops clipped."

The guy begrudgingly grumbles,
"Umph." Then he phones the crypt.

He tells us, "Cool your heels.
It'll be a little while.

Relax. Enjoy yourself, honey."
He leers at Jolene with a smirky smile.

Donald Dean Jackson

RIP – January 7th, 1966, Age 25
Killed by detective, Roland Charles.

The Fohrman Motors killings were covered by **Ebony** and **Jet**, two Chicago based magazines, whose primary market is the African American community. The January 27, 1966 issue of **Jet** reported that a Chicago alderman along with an Illinois state legislator were seeking to pass laws to protect citizens from usury loans with unreasonably high interest rates. The April 1966 issue of **Ebony** highlighted the Fohrman killings in an article on the pitfalls of credit buying, as it can hide inflated prices and extra finance charges. Seventeen years later, in 1983, the above-mentioned legislator won the election for Mayor of Chicago. His name was **Harold Washington**. He was Chicago's first black mayor.

Two more guys enter.
They look like the Press.

I nudge Jolene.
"We don't wan'em stirrin' up a mess."

"Go to the ladies' room.
I'll knock when it's O.K.

With luck, in ten minutes,

they'll go away."

The guy got the call from the crypt

a bit later.

By then, the Press left. I got Jolene.
We went to the elevator.

Shelf – The vault in the morgue where individual bodies are kept.

The day's events
kept spinning kinda weird.

All the time, I'm thinking,

"What am I doing here?"

"I've no interest in a bullet-holed
body," I thought to myself.
"I'll just stay at the elevator
and not go to the shelf."

No luck. The aide rolled
the body gurney across the floor.

White sheet on top, the cart sat
in front of the elevator door.

Detectives Roland Charles

RIP – December 19, 1974, Age 45
Nine years after the Fohrman killings

Detective Charles, a quiet and reserved man, received an award for bravery for his heroism at Fohrman Motors. He also received additional citations for other acts of courage. Detective Charles was an African American. Two weeks prior to his death, perhaps as a premonition of his coming demise, Charles wrote a three-page testament that included his belief that, "Mine is a wasted life." His letter focused on institutionalized racism and how it had limited him from his earliest days. His fellow police officers were shocked to learn of this as Charles was well liked and never expressed anger.

Jolene looked at the cart.

I stared at my feet.

"Is this your brother?" the aide asked,

pulling off the sheet.

One detective nudged Jolene.
She needed to confirm.

The poor girl stared, transfixed.
Her jaw very firm.

Then she grabbed my arm.

Her eyes opened wide.

"Dennis, look at his face.

He hadn't lied.

Detective York Anderson

RIP – September 15, 1985, Age 53
Eighteen years after the Fohrman killings

Detective Anderson, similar to Detective Charles, was also an African American. He also received numerous awards for bravery. He was a former US Marine Corps Sergeant who had been wounded during the Korean War. In 1970, he was put in charge of the first regular police patrol in the notorious Cabrini-Green Complex shortly after two police officers had been executed by a sniper. Some time after the Fohrman killings, the Chicago Police promoted him to Sergeant.

He made me a promise.
It's just like he said:

No worry, Sis. I'll wear a smile

when I'm dead.'"

Jolene's comments forced me

to take a look,

Though viewing a bullet-riddled killer

left me a little shook.

Sure enough, Jackson was smiling.
I swear on a case of gin.

He was staring up at me.
His mouth one big grin.

Chicago has long had the reputation of being the land of the gun. It gained its gangster notoriety during the prohibition days of the 1920's when rival gangs fought to bring illegal booze to the thousands of factory workers who yearned for a cold beer after a long day of hard work.

Unfortunately, Chicago continues to be known as a murder capital. In 2016, the city averaged two murders a day, with guns being the weapons of choice.

Though it was 50 years ago,

that day's still part of my life.

Thinking back, I hope Jolene
has had no more strife.

Now, it all bounces back into my mind,

when I hear that Elvis song play,

About a man shot down in a Chicago
ghetto on a cold and gray day.

Elvis Presley recorded the song,

In The Ghetto

on January 20th, 1969. It was released in April 1969. The song was written by the singer and songwriter, Mac Davis and was originally entitled, ***The Vicious Circle***.

Many believe ***In the Ghetto*** played a significant role in Presley's 1969 return to popularity. Elvis died eight years later on August 16, 1977 at age 42.

As a young man dies . . . . . . another baby child is born in the ghetto.

ABOUT THE AUTHOR

Dennis M Keating has enjoyed a peripatetic lifestyle. His international perspective and eclectic enthusiasm for life come from his forty some years in Germany; Thailand; China and Hawaii.

For the last ten years, Keating and his wife, Sandy, have been living a quiet life in Waikiki. Normally, he can be found pounding his iMac keyboard, hiking the Diamond Head trail, or strolling with his wife at sunset along the sands of Waikiki.

Keating writes on a diverse range of topics. His books draw upon his multifarious interests and personal experiences. Most of his books are nonfiction.

Keating's Facebook page:
https://www.facebook.com/TheHonoluluGuy/
He is happy to Friend you on Facebook.

In 2016, Keating released - *The Olympics: An Unauthorized Unsanctioned History*

In 2017, Keating released
Poetry for Men - Action Adventure Murder is a compilation of Keating's five poetry books.

Charlie Whitman was a Friend of Mine.
The story of the Texas Tower Killer.

Ena Road. Murder and racism in Hawaii.

The Fulda Gap. A Cold War confrontation.

A Chicago Tale. A triple murder story.

Black Lahu. Opium, life and death in the Golden Triangle.

His email is **lostpuka@gmail.com**
His websites are:
GoldenSphere.com & **HonoluluGuy.com**

Keating owns all rights to the material in this book. For film rights, or for other reasons, please contact him.

www.ingramcontent.com/pod-product-compliance
Lightning Source LLC
Chambersburg PA
CBHW071342290326
41933CB00040B/2086